Grateful
for You

Written by: M.H. Clark
Illustrated by: Cécile Metzger

This morning, I sat down to write out a list
of some of the things I'm most grateful exist—
the small things that change life in very big ways
by bringing their magic to regular days.

Like sweetly spiced cider in favorite mugs,
and sweaters that wrap you in all-day-long hugs...

And candles that flicker with soft, cozy light,
and stories that keep you up reading at night.

And trees with their leaves turning rust, red, and gold,
and thick scarves to bundle you up in the cold...

Watching fast-moving clouds in a blue autumn sky,
then hurrying home for a warm slice of pie...

As this list of my favorite things grew and it grew,
I found myself thinking a lot about you.

Because while these are things that I'm so grateful for,
I realized I'm grateful for *you* even more.

Because no mug of cider is sweeter than you,
and a hug from you beats any sweater (it's true).

And while candles and books are incredibly nice,
it's nicer by far to have you in my life.

And the truth is that bright leaves and crisp autumn air
would be just that much better if you were right there...

Do you know why there's more than one slice in a pie?

It's so there will be extra when you stop on by...

'Cause the bright things are brighter, the sweet things more sweet when you are a part of the moment with me.

I just know that each thing on my gratitude list
would be nicer with you there, to savor it with.

It's one of the most brilliant things about you:
you make the best parts of each good thing shine through.

Which is why, though I'm thankful for all of life's gifts, *you're* the one who most shows me what thankfulness is.

You remind me that good things exist everywhere,
and that they get better whenever they're shared.

There's a richness to life only friendship can bring...
maybe *that* is the secret to everything.

This morning, I sat down to write out a list
of some of the things I'm most grateful exist.
But the thing I'm most grateful for isn't a thing...
it's *you*, and the everyday magic you bring.

For wherever I go, and whatever I do,
I'm always most grateful when I'm there with you.

COMPENDIUM®
live inspired

Written by: M.H. Clark
Illustrated by: Cécile Metzger
Edited by: Bailey Vega
Art Directed by: Chelsea Bianchini

ISBN: 978-1-957891-29-3

1st printing. Printed in China with soy inks on FSC®-Mix certified paper.

Create meaningful moments with gifts that inspire.

CONNECT WITH US
live-inspired.com | sayhello@compendiuminc.com

   @compendiumliveinspired
#compendiumliveinspired